For over twenty-five years the early morning current affairs programme 'Today', now something of a radio phenomenon, has been delighting listeners with its subtle ability to mix 'hard' news with lighter items. A cabinet minister may well be followed by a granny who has just taken up karate, or a bishop by a chap who is riding round the world on a monocycle.

As co-presenter, John Timpson has been the programme's anchor for almost half its existence. It is he who tended to cover the more light-hearted pieces and who coined the phrase for the thirty-second filler which has become universally known as the 'ho-ho'. Enhanced by Bernard Cookson's witty drawings, this splendidly humorous collection of all the most amusing items broadcast includes some behind-the-scenes episodes, chapters on animal stories, inventions, record-breakers, eccentrics and the embarrassing accidents that have inevitably befallen John Timpson on the programme.

D0353736

The Lighter Side Of Today

JOHN TIMPSON
THE LIGHTER SIDE OF
TODAY

Illustrated by Bernard Cookson

London
UNWIN PAPERBACKS
Boston   Sydney

First published in Great Britain by George Allen & Unwin 1983
First published by Unwin Paperbacks 1985

UNWIN ® PAPERBACKS
40 Museum Street, London WC1A 1LU, UK

Unwin Paperbacks
Park Lane, Hemel Hempstead, Herts HP2 4TE, UK

Allen & Unwin Inc.,
Fifty Cross Street, Winchester, Mass 01890, USA

George Allen & Unwin Australia Pty Ltd.,
8 Napier Street, North Sydney, NSW 2060, Australia

Unwin Paperbacks with the Port Nicholson Press
PO Box 11–838 Wellington, New Zealand

Text © John Timpson 1983, 1985
Illustrations © Bernard Cookson 1983, 1985

ISBN 0 04 791044 5

Set in 11 on 12 point Souvenir by V & M Graphics, Aylesbury, Bucks
and printed in Great Britain by
Cox & Wyman Ltd, Reading

Contents

Preface

'Today' is essentially a news and current affairs programme. It is compiled and presented by professional journalists and its object is to report the news and views of the morning more quickly, more efficiently and more accurately than its competitors, whether they be newspapers, other radio stations or, more recently, breakfast television. But successive editors and those above them quickly appreciated that an unleavened loaf of 'hard' news for up to two and a half hours at breakfast time would be far too indigestible for most stomachs. A little yeast is needed to give it some lightness and lift, even the occasional inconsequential bubble.

The tricky part, of course, is to get the mixture right. Sometimes it can be too frothy, sometimes too leaden. But a mixture there must be: 'Today' would long since have ceased without yeast.

It comes in many forms, sometimes planned, sometimes spontaneous, sometimes entirely accidental. In a live programme such moments can be as disconcerting for the presenters as they are entertaining for the listeners. There are many mornings when we start the programme wondering how we shall ever wade through it, and miraculously something lifts it to provide some sparkle after all.

This is what *The Lighter Side Of Today* is all about. It would be equally possible to compile *The More Serious Side Of Today*, but you could find the same material on the front pages of the papers, in the comment columns of the news magazines, scattered across the business sections and the financial weeklies. It is in short just 'the news'. The lighter side is that extra ingredient which makes 'Today' a more palatable breakfast serial, for those who listen to it and indeed for the 'Today' team which provides it.

J.T.

1 The 'Ho-Ho' – A Definitive Study

The 'ho-ho' started on the 'Today' programme in the early 'seventies as an innocuous way of filling a spare twenty seconds; by the early 'eighties it had developed almost into a cult. It provoked the longest-running correspondence in the history of the programme. It drove listeners to inordinate lengths to find a ho-ho in a new context or a new continent. Photographs, leaflets, match folders, lapel badges, even planks of wood poured into the 'Today' office, all bearing the ho-ho emblem in some unlikely form. It even achieved that final mark of respectability, a mention in 'Thought for the Day'. This, then, is the ho-ho story.

It is our practice on 'Today', when a tape recording ends too early, or a guest fails to appear, or there is less weather about than usual, to while away the empty moments by quoting some ambiguous headline or unlikely misprint or eccentrically worded ad. We are not saying anything of any significance, we are merely making some sort of noise so listeners know that their radios have not broken down. It may be a letter someone has received from British Telecom, signed by a Miss Busby; an order of service for a wedding bearing the advice, 'During the signing of the Register, Sheep May Safely Graze'; or, more daringly, a rare example of levity in a *Financial Times* headline, 'INSULATION: BRITAIN LAGS BEHIND'.

The more painful of these offerings were followed up with an apologetic 'ho ho', and thus the exasperating little expression was born. Like housey-housey or Morecambe and Wise, it was around for years before it caught on. Then, as it gathered momentum, it virtually took on a life of its own – and it almost took over the programme as well.

It started with a listener's letter advising us that he had come upon a town in West Africa called Ho Ho. When I was foolhardy enough to quote it, the senior lecturer in town and country planning at Bristol Polytechnic confirmed that, while working with his students on the distribution of road densities in Ghana, 'we discovered that a pocket of particularly high-network density extended inland from Ho to Hohoe.' And we were off.

An old Africa hand discounted the discovery. While the spelling was right, or near enough, the pronunciation was wrong. Hohoe actually sounded like Hoch-we. As a consolation, however, he offered us another Hho Hho in Swaziland. This was forthwith ruled out by a South African listener who pointed out that the 'ho' in this instance had a short 'o', as in 'shop'. But by now it was too late to stop the ho-ho flow.

A gentleman in the Commonwealth Secretariat at Marlborough House told us about the suburb of Port Moresby in Papua New Guinea called Hohola. A veteran of the Fourteenth Army recalled a railway station in the Shan States of Burma called Heho (where, presumably, it's off to work they go). We learned of a Mexican village called Xo-Xo – pronounced, of course, Ho-Ho. And several people with trans-Atlantic connections told us about the town in New Jersey, of Red Indian origin, with the endearing name of Ho-Ho-Cus, which prompted the thought that if they manufactured fire-irons there they could call them Ho-Ho-Cus Pokers.

While the gazetteers and atlases were being milked dry of ho-ho material, other listeners were seeking inspiration from their local high streets and their holiday snaps. Pictures poured in of Ho Ho Chinese laundries, Ho Ho takeaways, Ho Ho toyshops, from Hemel Hempstead to Hong Kong. A photograph taken off the coast of Kenya showed a magnificent dhow bearing the name 'Hoho'. Somewhere in Malaysia a listener had spotted a van bearing the legend 'Ho Ho the Biscuit Factory', which fitted perfectly, he pointed out, the chorus of 'Scotland the Brave'. And so it does – the 'Today' office rang with it all day! One snapshot of a Chinese restaurant in Doncaster was accompanied by this amiable version of 'Captain Beaky':

> The intrepid Timpson and his band
> Are searching high and low
> The length and breadth of many a land
> To find a new ho-ho.
> Why go to Patagonia or outer Katmandu?
> There's one in God's own county
> And we snapped it just for you.

◈ ◈ ◈

Mr Booker of Farnham sent us some poetry, too, but in this case it was by no less than Edward Thomas. The first verse of Thomas' poem 'The Cuckoo', runs:

> That's the cuckoo, you say. I cannot hear it.
> When last I heard it I cannot recall; but I know
> Too well the year when first I failed to hear it –
> It was drowned by my man groaning out to his sheep
> 'Ho! Ho!'

Mr Booker also quoted a reference from Evelyn Waugh's *Diaries* for May 1956: 'Whit Monday at breakfast R. A.

Butler arrived, squinny-eyed, awkward, given to horrible outbursts of "Yo ho ho".'

Some of our correspondents began to speak in foreign tongues. A former East African planter told us that the Swahili word for pepper was pili-pili, and very hot pepper was known as pili-pili ho ho, 'the ho ho being emphasised by indrawn breath, as when one pops something uncomfortably hot in the mouth'.

Indian braves, it seems, are ho-ho-ing constantly, though the ho can be confused with the more familiar 'How!'

The curator of the South Wales Borderers Museum sent us a drawing from an 1879 *Illustrated London News* at the time of the Zulu war with the caption: 'General Lord Chelmsford reviewing the native contingent on the banks of the Tugela, the natives shouting "H-H-HOOO!"'

And during the Falklands conflict an ex-Gurkha officer advised us that the Gurkhas on board the QE2 were doubtless indulging in their traditional dances which end with cries of not just 'Ho Ho' but 'Ho Ho Ho Ho Ho ...'

Now we were entering new fields of ho-ho erudition. An honorary professor in Ancient Oriental Studies sent us a mini-treatise on the place of 'ho' and 'ho ho' in Chinese culture, dating back to the Tang Dynasty (AD 620–907), when the Emperor Chang An was named Ho by his people. This meant, he claimed, that a new hotel in Peking called the Chang Ho could equally be called the Ho Ho. It was not until the Ming Dynasty, he added, that the two words were regularly used together. At that time, he assured us, Ho Ho meant the auburn scalp of a fellow-worker. By now we were believing almost anything.

Another learned correspondent, a don in the geography department of the Queen's University, Belfast, advised us that the Hawaiian term for 'ropy or corded volcanic lava' was pahoehoe. Significantly perhaps, it is pronounced pahooey-hooey.

The up-market trend continued. Ho ho featured in an *Observer* colour supplement crossword. The clue was: 'Two useless pubs, that's funny (4 letters)'. In crossword terms pub equals house, and a house which was without use was ho. Thus, ho ho. It was also pointed out to me that, perhaps appropriately since the stuff flows fairly freely at times on 'Today', the chemical formula for adrenalin starts 'HO HO ...'.

Much information came in about the Chinese ho ho bird, a mixture of flamingo, peacock and parrot we were told, to be found in stately homes from Sussex (Petworth) to Somerset (Montacute House). Of rather less distinguished pedigree was the jojoba bean (pronounced hohoba), which featured in some powerful advertising as the answer to pretty well all the needs of mankind, though so far it seems to have surfaced commercially only as a face-oil.

To balance this, however, we were reminded by a lady in Brighton with a sound working knowledge of the Buddha-Karita of Asvaghosa: 'Having attained the highest wisdom, Buddha mounted on a throne up in the air to a height of seven palm trees and declared, "Ho ho! Listen ye to the words of me who has now attained perfect knowledge!"'

The final ecclesiastical accolade came from one of our 'Thought for the Day' contributors who found an excuse for quoting the second chapter of Zechariah, verse six: 'Ho, ho, come forth, and flee from the land of the north, saith the Lord' – directed, no doubt, at Geordie Brian Redhead.

Having traced the ho-ho back to the Old Testament, where was there left to go? Some listeners, verging on desperation, sent in entire pages of telephone directories – 'The A to Z of the Dial-a-Ho-Ho Industry' as one described them. The London list included one festive Ho who called his house Holly Ho; surprisingly, there was no Ho listed in Soho. But a learned professor at Manchester University took the trouble to write to us while on vacation in the Far East to advise us that the Singapore directory contained a Mr Ho whose first name was Wat.

A Woolwich resident noted that there was a Ha Ha Street in the otherwise unfrivolous environs of the Army Academy. A lady from Singapore told us she used to employ an amah to look after the children whose name was Ho Lai Har and who, in accordance with Cantonese custom, was known as Ah Har. 'She could never understand why the children thought it so funny.'

The most unusual contribution to the correspondence was a piece of plank bearing the simple inscription 'OH HO'. It was the shipping mark of a well-known Finnish timber exporter. All over the world, it was pointed out, there must be wooden buildings displaying this tribute to what was fast becoming a national fetish. But this, said the sender, overcome by ho-ho mania, this must be the last wood on the subject.

Wood that it was. (Is there no escape?) But the correspondence still continues, the hohobilia still accumulates. At Christmas there will be the usual crop of cards for the 'Today' office displaying jolly Santas and their traditional Yuletide greeting, and paper napkins covered with the ubiquitous cry. Already a new generation is being born: I have had the first photograph of the son of Ho Ho, a fish-and-chip shop in Rhyl called the T.Yee.

◇ ◇ ◇

'... traced the ho-ho back to the Old Testament ...'

My colleagues sometimes get a little exasperated by it all. We do deal primarily with the serious world about us, yet even on something like the Pope's visit we get letters asking if he travels in a pontificart or a hoholicopter. But let us not be ungrateful. I particularly treasure a little drawing I received of the genial philosopher, Nastidin-Hohojar, who travelled around Asia Minor in the Middle Ages cheering up the populace with merry little tales. Whether or not, wrote the sender, his name reflects the reception his stories received, the legend is that no-one remains serious for long when his replica hangs on the wall.

It hangs on my wall even now – and it still seems to work.

2 'Can You Come In And Do It Live?'

It is amazing how often you can. On the debit side there is the early rise, the strange environment, the odd characters who are likely to receive you. On the credit side there is the cup of BBC coffee, you have beaten the rush hour, and if you have an axe to grind, a cause to promote or just a line to shoot, you have the biggest radio current affairs audience of the day. Be prepared, though, for the unexpected.

The radio and television critic, Chris Dunkley, one of our occasional contributors, described our old waiting room (or 'Hospitality Room' as it was ludicrously called) as having all the welcoming cosiness of a meat safe. He was being too generous. Apart from the bleak furnishings and the claustrophobic lack of windows, a large and menacing mirror covered the whole of one wall. Few people look or feel their best at seven in the morning, but to have it proved by that mirror that you are not one of them was an ordeal nobody should have to endure. Fortunately the room became so congested at peak times with guests, producers, studio managers and the occasional itinerant electrician that there was little chance for any lengthy self-examination.

The only improvement on the average dentist's waiting room was that at least the newspapers were up to date. On the whole, however, there must have been for the uninitiated the same atmosphere of impending doom, the same dread of the eventual summons to the room across

19

'... a large and menacing mirror covered the whole of one wall.'

the corridor, as they grasped their plastic cups, avoided their own eyes in the mirror and tried not to jog the arm of the Cabinet minister in the next seat.

For the entertainment of those who awaited our pleasure, there was for many years the 'Today' ducking stool. This was an evilly-designed armless sofa on which one set of legs was placed much too close to the centre, so that any weight applied to the extreme end resulted in the legs acting as a fulcrum and the sofa turning into a see-saw. This did not matter as long as somebody was already sitting on the other end, but as soon as that counterweight was removed, the whole contraption tilted sideways and the unfortunate victim was dumped ignominiously on the floor.

Some distinguished notches were carved on the ducking stool in its time: at least one Northern Ireland Secretary, a couple of bishops, a wide range of trade union leaders, top industrialists and backbenchers (or flatbenchers as we liked to picture them on these occasions). If they happened to be grasping a cup of tea at the time, that counted as bonus points. The enormous mirror, incidentally, was so placed that the victim could actually see himself descending, an added refinement which must have added vastly to his discomfiture.

Some spoilsport removed the sofa after a while, before any bones were broken or any egos too badly damaged. As I write there are plans to dispense with the Hospitality Room also, in favour of more elegant premises. We shall have to devise some other softening-up process for our more complacent guests.

Across the corridor in Studio 3E, the home of the 'Today' programme for many years, the chairs are more reliable but can often be in too great demand. There are only five around our D-shaped table – two along the straight side for the presenters, three on the curved side for everybody else.

21

As the news bulletins are read in the same studio, this can cause considerable congestion at certain points in the programme. Interviewees have to lurk around the walls until chairs are vacated by the newsreader and the newsroom sub-editor who acts as 'minder', and when the introduction to the live interview is fairly brief there is a hasty bout of silent musical chairs as Pauline Bushnell or Peter Donaldson scrambles out and Sir Geoffrey Howe or Roy Hattersley scrambles in. The whole operation has to be carried out on tiptoe and in complete silence, giving it all a surreal and dream-like effect.

The traffic does not stop there. Sports reporters appear and disappear, the 'Thought for the Day' thinker manoeuvres for position, secretaries putter in with a motoring flash or a late headline or just a further supply of tea. Frequently a live interview has to continue throughout all these exits and entrances, and it must be very difficult for an inexperienced guest to concentrate on questions about the Green Pound or the economic recession in West Germany or the American nuclear missile programme while a ghostly army flits silently in and out.

Not that they are always that silent. There was the morning when the Deputy Editor of 'Today' fell heavily over a metal wastepaper basket during the course of a live interview. There was another when the newsreader and his colleague came into the studio, chatting cheerfully, while we were introducing the weather forecast. And how often has the studio door been opened just as the tea trolley is rattling past, or a great burst of laughter has gushed out from the Hospitality Room across the way.

If the professionals can slip up like this, small wonder some of our guests get caught out too.

It is not unusual at the end of an interview for the guest to be so relieved the ordeal is over that he leaps immediately to his feet and crashes out of the door. This can be much more disastrous on television, when not only can he be seen as well as heard, but he may also strangle himself with his neck-mike. Even on radio, it can cause quite a disturbance.

My most memorable experience of this kind was with a distinguished professor, a great expert on some subject so obscure that I have quite forgotten what it was. He had arrived a little late and had been whisked out of his taxi, through the foyer, into the lift, along the corridor (by-passing the Hospitality Room) and straight into the studio. There was no time for explanation or preparation. As soon as he sat down we started the interview, and to his lasting credit he answered the questions with great clarity and aplomb. At the end of it I thanked him and led him to the door. Robert Robinson, the other presenter at that time, started to introduce the next item.

It had all happened in such a whirl, though, that I suspect the good professor had no idea he had actually been broadcasting. Perhaps he thought we had just been having a preliminary chat in some back room. I had got him as far as the door when suddenly he stopped dead, went back to the table, lent over Bob's shoulder and enquired, a few inches from the microphone, 'Excuse me. Did you see where I left my hat?' The whole nation started looking for it.

There are many more live interviews in the programme than there used to be. It gives the programme greater immediacy and spontaneity, but it creates a lot more problems as well. It is rare for a guest to dry up completely, though there have been occasions when the questions have had to get longer and longer as the answers got shorter and shorter. When the only response is a nod, you know it is time to give up. The more usual difficulty is getting people to stop.

It is not so bad if they are in the studio with you. You can make gestures and grimaces and as a last resort you can always put a bag over their head. It is more tricky with interviews 'down the line', when the guest can be on the other side of the country or the other side of the world, not appreciating that vital seconds are ticking away and the nation is agog for the weather forecast.

In these cases the only device is a nervous cough or a grunt or even an impatient 'yes, yes', to indicate a certain restlessness at the receiving end. On only one occasion did we reach such desperate straits that we actually faded somebody out in mid-flow – a BBC correspondent at that. As so often happens, the final question was intended to produce only a crisp yes or no. Instead he embarked on a lengthy tirade which began to encroach further and further onto the space allotted to 'Thought for the Day'. Even blunt interruptions and cries of 'Thank you' and 'Splendid' and 'That's fine' failed to stop the flow. Looking back, we should probably have cut him off completely and pretended the line had gone down. As it was, he faded gradually into the distance. We could still hear him as we introduced 'Thought for the Day'. For all I know, he is talking still.

If a contributor cannot get to the 'Today' studio to be interviewed, various alternatives are available. He may be near one of our regional studios, where the local staff can look after him. Rather trickier are our unattended studios, which are scattered throughout the country in the most unlikely situations. There is one above a dentist's surgery, another at the back of a public library, a third in a town hall and so on. Each one has its printed set of instructions and everything is made as simple as possible, but it can still be a daunting experience to be tucked away in one of these isolated rooms, often in an otherwise deserted building, with only a disembodied voice in the headphones for company and knowing that whatever you say will be heard by millions.

There is one of these studios in particular which I shall

always recall with a shiver. It was in the top room of an old country vicarage, close to the church but not much else. It so happened that the vicar and his family were on holiday and the house was empty. It was midwinter, a wild night with the rain pelting down and the wind howling. I crept up the creaking stairs to the little studio under the eaves, got the equipment working, made contact with Broadcasting House and started sending my report.

Mercifully it was not going out live, because in the middle of it, as I sat in my lonely eyrie, three shadowy storeys up in that deserted Victorian pile, there was a sudden loud bang on the window. 'Aaaah!' I cried, to the astonishment of the engineer at the other end, who thought I had pressed the wrong button and electrocuted myself. Indeed, the shock was very similar. The noise had been just a branch blowing against the window, but it was some time before I could get the quaver out of my voice to finish the report.

If our contributor lives within thirty miles or so of Portland Place but is still disinclined to make the journey, we can use the radio car, but this too presents its problems. Not unnaturally, casual passers-by can be quite fascinated by the sight of a government minister in his dressing gown and slippers, sitting in the back of what looks a cross between a taxi and a telegraph pole. The very high mast on the roof does rather attract attention, and it cannot be easy to concentrate on a conversation with an unseen interviewer while a crowd of spectators gathers around the windows.

At least these days they are not likely to suffer the same disaster that is said to have overtaken one of our earlier radio cars, which were just ordinary saloons with an expanding aerial on the boot. One such car was parked facing up a fairly steep hill. The distinguished contributor was ushered into it and the engineer wound up the heavy aerial to its full extent – whereupon the car gently toppled over backwards.

It is not only the outside end of an outside link that can have its problems. We once had a sports reporter, who shall remain mercifully nameless, who was in the 'Today' studio monitoring the progress of a Test match in Australia. He was listening to the commentary on Radio 3, so that at an appropriate moment he could announce the score and a few details about the state of play. However, he became so engrossed in following the game that he quite forgot where he was. All unsuspecting, I announced, 'Let's see how the Test match is going. What's the latest score?' Our listeners were treated to the crisp reply: 'Do shut up – I'm trying to listen!'

When a morning is really busy, one can run into another problem over interviews with unseen guests, the problem of mistaken identity. Often there is no time for a chat before the interview starts, and we can slip up over wrong Christian names, wrong titles, wrong designations – and very occasionally, wrong people.

The most famous incident fortunately happened off the air. We were to record a talented gentleman who was able to play tunes under his armpits. The action, we understood, was rather similar to playing the bagpipes, but without the bag. The sounds came like a series of burps, and apparently he could adjust the note by placing his other hand in the armpit. It all sounded as if it ought to be another 'Today' winner. We made an appointment with him to come into one of our regional studios during the evening to do his stuff, and in due course the reporter was called into our studio at Broadcasting House to record the interview. What he did

'... whereupon the car gently toppled over backwards.'

not know was that another interviewee had been booked for the same regional studio, and had arrived first.

'Good evening,' said our reporter blithely. 'Before we actually start the interview, would you just play us a tune under your armpit?'

There was the slightest of pauses at the other end, then a voice said apologetically, 'I'll do my best, but what does that have to do with the Common Market Fishery policy?'

Eccentric musicians are a favourite feature of live interviews on 'Today'. We always enjoy the chap who can make a wind instrument out of a kettle and a length of garden hose. We once entertained a man who could tap out the 'William Tell' Overture on his teeth, an agonising performance which set less musical molars aching in mouths all over the nation. Even more painful was the RAF sergeant who played 'Rule Britannia' by hitting himself on the head with a nine-inch spanner. We took the precaution of interviewing him first in case he was a bit groggy afterwards, but as it turned out he even gave us an encore.

One expects problems with this sort of dotty performer, but the worst ones have actually occurred with more orthodox musicians. We ended the programme one morning with a Hungarian virtuoso who had little grasp of the English language, but a very firm grasp indeed on his violin. We had asked him to give us a short sample of his skill, but obviously he did not know the meaning of 'short' and unfortunately we did not know the Hungarian for 'stop!'

The closing headlines, the weather forecast, all the usual farewell civilities went by the board as our guest scraped away into the microphone, oblivious of the growing hysteria all about him. Long after we had been faded off the air and the next programme was well into its stride, he was still at it. He only stopped when we brought in his agent and told him that was as far as our money went.

Over the years we have managed to accommodate double basses, tubas, even a complete string quartet in our rather cramped studio. The one instrument that beat us was an alpenhorn. This monstrous device, some ten or twelve feet long, is admirably suited to an Alp but quite the wrong design for our studio. We compromised by having the bell end inside the studio with us, while the alpenhornist stood in the corridor to blow down the other.

This required a complex system of signals via an intermediary, as the player was actually out of our sight. Such a system was duly arranged, and after as many blasts on his alpenhorn as we thought the listeners could stand, we sent him the signal to stop. To our relief, he did – or so we thought. Only when we were halfway through announcing 'Thought for the Day' did he play his final deafening, Alp-shattering note, a combination of a trumpeting elephant and the siren on the QE2. It gave the thought for that day a most remarkable send-off.

It is very pleasant, incidentally, to have a live contributor so frequently these days in 'Thought for the Day'. There was a time when the 'Thought' was always sent over in advance by the Religious Broadcasting Department in the form of a tape recording, perhaps because in those days our religious broadcasters did not get up terribly early – rumour had it that they only just made it for Morning Service at half-past ten. But in recent times we have welcomed a very distinguished selection of speakers to the studio: bishops and abbots, a lady Rabbi, a prison governor, welfare workers, charity organisers – and the charming Rosemary Hartill.

Rosemary is the BBC's religious affairs correspondent, and is one of our regular contributors. I always feel we have a sort of special relationship since we spent several hours early one morning closeted in a tiny commentary box in the middle of Gatwick airport for the arrival of the Pope. We spent a desperate ten minutes between the time the plane landed and the time it actually taxied to a halt, Rosemary giving the history of every Pontiff since St Peter and I describing each individual oil stain on the tarmac. That sort of experience must forge a lasting link.

Anyway, Brian Redhead thinks so, and he capitalised on it one morning in a way which nearly produced a broadcasting disaster. Rosemary had joined us in the studio a few minutes before 'Thought' was due, and while the tape before it was running, Brian announced suddenly, 'I had an amazing dream last night.'

'Tell us about it,' I said, knowing he would anyway.

'I dreamed', he said, 'I had gone to Heaven. St Peter met me at the gate and checked his records and said, as a penance for my activities down here, I would spend the next seven years in Heaven shackled to a terrible old whisky-sodden crone. This didn't seem too severe, all things considered, so off I hobbled with this crone attached to me – only to see Timpson wandering about Heaven, shackled to Rosemary Hartill.

'I forthwith went back to St Peter to complain. "Here I am," I said, landed with this frightful smelly old crone, and there is Timpson shackled to Rosemary Hartill. Whereupon St Peter said, "You get on with your penance and let Rosemary Hartill get on with hers."'

Brian had just finished when the green light went on, the microphone was live, and I had to announce to the nation, 'Here is "Thought for the Day", with Rosemary Hartill.' I shall never know how I got through it.

3 Animals That Ran And Ran

It is no secret that the British are crackers about animals. The little chaps do not need to be charming or cuddly or the remotest bit cute. As long as they look defenceless, whether they waddle or wriggle or just lie there, they can be assured of our care and affection. Over the years 'Today' listeners have involved themselves in the affairs of the hedgehog, the earthworm, the bee and the shoat. The shoat? Well, it could be a geep.

The average hedgehog, surrounded by prickles and infested with fleas, has no obvious attractions except perhaps for another hedgehog. Yet when the British Hedgehog Preservation Society revealed on the programme one morning that it was launching a campaign to instal ramps under cattle grids as an escape route for hedgehogs which had fallen through the bars, the response was staggering. The nation was swept by an enormous protectiveness towards hedgehogs. Why stop at cattle grids, they cried? What about hedgehog gullies across motorways, hedgehog warning lights for night drivers, hedgehog barriers around garden swimming pools?

It was the pool protection problem which produced the most correspondence. Long after the first ramps had been installed in two Shropshire cattle grids, listeners were still pondering the prickly problem of keeping hedgehogs out of their pools. An entire class at Burnbush Primary School in

Bristol sent in illustrated ideas for keeping the little fellows on dry land. They ranged from a radio-controlled model train circling the pool, driven by a toy hedgehog announcing in hedgehog language 'Keep out!', to a sprung platform working on a reverse moustrap principle, so that when a hedgehog stepped onto it the spring flew up and flung him backwards – 'into a comfortable bush', as the youthful designer described it.

A more practical solution came from a Mr Johnson of Felixstowe, who suggested that where hedgehogs had gone wrong was to rely on inflatable life jackets, which for a hedgehog were manifestly impractical. Foam-filled jackets were the obvious answer.

An imaginative gentleman from Diss in Norfolk went a stage further. He claimed to have seen a hedgehog wearing a life jacket and carrying a stepladder. 'I take this,' he said, 'to be a remarkable example of communication among the species, since there are neither swimming pools nor cattle grids within several miles of here. On the other hand, you could have a huge and prickly audience of which you were previously unaware!'

A more erudite contribution came from a Mr O'Connor of the history of art department at the University of Manchester. It was a postcard produced by the Swedish Post Office in 1914 displaying an apprehensive hedgehog fleeing across a road with the caption which Mr O'Connor translated as 'In summer be careful of hedgehogs in the traffic.'

It was a kindly thought which not all our listeners shared. All the dreadful hedgehog jokes poured in. 'Why did the hedgehog cross the road? To see a flat mate.' 'How do you score 800 at darts with one throw? Throw a hedgehog.' We were going downhill fast.

The situation was retrieved finally by a delightful tale from a Miss Peterkin of Lyme Regis, who recalled that during a winter blizzard, while putting out the milk bottles late at night, a kindly soul saw a little hedgehog huddling in the snow. Forthwith she heated a saucer of milk and put it beside the poor creature. Next morning she found a saucerful of iced milk, and a frozen lavatory brush.

About the same time as the Great Hedgehog Debate we uncovered the Earthworm Lobby. The support for the worm dates back to Charles Darwin, who had many kind things to say about this apparently unattractive creature and its contribution to our ecology. We foolishly made light of this very serious tribute, and received this reprimand from Mr Ewan Clarkson of Newton Abbot:

Mock not the earthworm, that truly noble beast,
Custodian of our native soil, to say the very least.
It burrows down and down and down,
And then comes squirming back
To shed a little casting
In a neatly coiled up pack.

It's working while you're sleeping, lad,
To fertilise the land,
Ten pounds a year of compost rare –
Now don't you think that's grand?

There's nitrogen and potash too, and phosphorous galore,
Spread at your feet, all nice and neat, and always plenty more.
And all for free, so don't you see how good worms are to you.
So please confirm, you'll be friends with a worm in 1982.

More letters came in. A visitor to Oslo told us that a pamphlet in his hotel, under the heading 'Theatres – Musicals – Revues', featured a talk at the National Theatre called 'Fra regnormenes liv' – From the Life of the Earthworms. Unfortunately, he did not attend it. But many more odes and tributes came from 'Today' wormophiles and the ingenious Mr Clarkson, by now the self-styled head of SPEW, the Society for the Protection of Earthworms, rounded off the correspondence with another earthy contribution:

A torrid tale of the earthworm, for your interest and delight,
About what goes on, on your own back lawn, in the middle of the night.
When the dew lies white on the new-mown grass and the woody owl calls soft,
Each impatient worm gives an amorous squirm and hauls itself aloft.
Up a long dark tunnel from the bowels of the earth
It climbs to the stars above,
With each wriggle and writhe every worm's alive
With the burning fires of love.
Then once outside with a slither and a slithe, and every worm takes part,
There's a slippery race to a slimy embrace with the object of its heart.
Now love is blind as you'll agree, and worms are blind and dumb,
Yet they find delight in the middle of the night – now don't you think that's rum?
The secret now I'll breathe to you, how worms find ecstasy,
For every worm that's born to squirm is wired AC/DC.
And in a word, though it seems absurd, they are bound to get it right,
For every lover that goes after another is a true hermaphrodite.

The Earthworm Lobby was eventually crowded out by the Bee Brigade. We passed on an appeal from a lady bee-lover who suggested that, if one came upon an apparently deceased specimen on the kitchen window sill it might well be revived with a drop of honey left nearby. It transpired, however, that according to many experts honey is bad for bees; a little sugared water was the answer. But this did not stop our correspondents from once again bursting into verse. One contribution was sent to us by the nephew of Sir

Geoffrey Vickers, holder of the VC, author of such learned works as *Value Systems and Social Process*, a wartime deputy director-general at the Ministry of Economic Welfare but, in the midst of all these dazzling distinctions, it appeared, a lover of bees. He wrote this when he was already in his seventies. There was time to quote only a brief excerpt on the programme, but here it is, complete:

Blinds up, pure light flooded the kitchen.
Sink, cooker and kettle shone bright as a new creation:
Even I, half assured of a new beginning.
But there on the sill's bright white expanse,
A dead bee curled, shrivelled, colour of ash,
Denied the dawn, the hush of a world's renewal.
My home his trap? Shame dulled the light to common day.
Not mine to undo death. In expiation
I dropped a gold bead from a syrup jar by the bee's nose.
I moved him close. I waited, respecting transience,
Not awaiting a miracle.
Silence deepened. I felt sweet scent beat on his stilled nerves;
But he could not hear, could not answer.
Life called, called, but he did not move. Then
I sensed a change. I watched, watched, waited.
Time stilled. The world emptied. Only the bee was there.
Minutes passed.
Then slowly, slowly outstretched a black proboscis to touch
    the drop.
From its tip a tongue extended, tiny, golden, curved,
A sickle weakly circling. Nothing in all the world
Moved but the bee's tongue.
                    Then, O then
Each dried hair glowed golden or black,
A live bee, vibrant, poised on vigorous feet,
Dizzy with energy, drunk with life,
Pulling his nose free, zooming round the ceiling,
A bee possessed by zest for unfinished business.
A bee away through the open window, steering by the sun
For the hive and the day's work.

The kitchen, stilled of his hum, fell quiet,
As when first, blinds up, pure light flooded sink, cooker and
  kettle.
Even I, more than half assured of a new beginning.

The bee story with the best sting in the tail came from a Mr
John Mottram of Edinburgh, who recalled taking an elderly
lady out to tea in Princes Street. She thought it would be
nice to have honey instead of jam on her scones, and the
honey was duly brought – in the kind of little plastic box that
some less discerning restaurants indulge in. She studied the
offering and then, in a voice that Lady Bracknell would have
envied, she announced to the delight of everyone in ear-
shot (which must have been most of Princes Street), 'I
obser-r-r-ve you keep a bee.'

And the shoats?
   It was an interview with a West Country lady who milked
her sheep that started the correspondence on this hybrid
animal, which was such an odd mixture that it was difficult
to tell the geep from the shoats. A Mrs Currey of
Hampshire, who spent some time in Malta, recalled how the
'milkman' brought his herd of shoats down the main street,
'dropping manure as they went.... Some udders hung to
the ground while others were encased in primitive bras.
Housewives would lower a basket on a string from an upper
window, with the money and a container for the milk. The
shoats were duly milked and the herd went on its way, still
fouling the streets.' (Mrs Currey obviously felt strongly
about this.) She added, 'For the Forces families like us this
milk was forbidden, for fear of "Malta Fever". The warning
was quite unnecessary.'
   All this was confirmed by Mr Joseph Ross of Sidmouth,
who added that once the animals had yielded all their milk

'The shoats were duly milked and the herd went on its way ...'

they were turned into mutton. And once again a poem appeared, this time from the bottom of his 'dittybox', where it had lurked for forty years. He called it 'The Maltese Cross'.

> The Maltese, I'm told, cross goats with sheep.
> The hybrid beasts, called shoats (or geep?)
> Yield milk like goats and, like sheep, meat.
> How neat! I wonder if they 'blaa' or 'beet'?

◇　◇　◇

Finally, it would be a pity to leave out the letter from an eminent firm of chartered patent agents and European patent attorneys in Kent, who informed us about their latest client, a pigeon. This enterprising bird claimed to have invented the first all-steel nest, which it had assembled on the window ledge of their gentlemen's cloakroom.

They described it as 'a plurality of twig-like elements of mild steel (16 standard wire gauge), each 6–8 inches in length. Presumably these have undergone aerial transportation from Messrs Taylor Woodrow, now building an office block nearby. The nest is durable, although not rust-proof, and can be dismantled for storage, like a plastic Christmas tree. It is obviously functional, since it contains one egg with the mother nesting upon it.'

They asked us not to mention the name of their firm, since they would not wish to attract other bird inventors, thereby risking a conflict of interests.

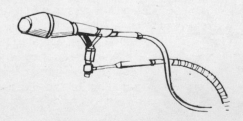

4 A Backward Glance At The Palindrome

Whenever a date comes round like 18 September 1981, we are invariably advised by some painstaking palindromaniac that it is reversible: 18.9.1981. Some people cheat a bit and argue that dates like 28.11.82 also qualify, though the perfectionists maintain that the numbers must look exactly the same backwards too. Thus you could have 11.8.1811–but not a lot else. However, palindromic dates also prompt listeners to produce palindromic sentences, and once we had quoted the odd example we found we had opened a veritable Palindora's Box.

'A man, a plan, a canal – Panama!' has always been the favourite, with Napoleon's forlorn observation, 'Able was I ere I saw Elba', a close runner-up. That greeting in the Garden of Eden, 'Madam, I'm Adam', with the confusing riposte, 'Sir, I'm Iris', comes a creditable third. But there is a strong following for two literary examples. Dr Johnson is attributed with the comment to a widow on learning that the deceased husband had bequeathed less to him than he had expected: 'Madame, not one man is selfless, I name not one, madam' – the spelling of 'madame' being adjusted to fit. And the Scottish poet, Alastair Reid, is supposed to have conjured up the ingenious if insanitary vignette: 'T. Eliot, top bard, notes putrid tang emanating, is sad. I'd assign it a name: gnat dirt upset on drab pot toilet.'

◇ ◇ ◇

The offerings which reached us were not only in English. Many correspondents quoted the Greek inscription at St Sophia's Cathedral, Constantinople, said to appear above a washbowl so that it could be read reflected in the water: 'Nispon anomimata mi monan opsin' – We must wash away the impiety, not merely the outward appearance. We were offered one in German: 'Ein neger mit gazelle zagt im regen nie' – A negro and a gazelle never hesitate in the rain. And most ingenious of all, a palindromic Latin square: 'Rotas opera tenet arepo sator'. Put the five words on top of each other and you can read them upwards and downwards as well as backwards and forwards.

We cannot claim any records for the palindromes we received. Indeed, I was abashed to receive a copy of the *New Statesman* published in 1967 which ran a competition for palindromes and printed hordes of them. They were not always very intelligible but some were of inordinate length, 150 words or more. The best of them, which earned the sender five guineas and has turned up often since, was: 'Doc, note, I dissent. A fast never prevents a fatness. I diet on cod.'

We did not attempt to compete with the *New Statesman*, but we did receive a couple which I particularly cherish. One consisted of an interminable list of names, over sixty of them, starting 'Dennis, Nell, Edna, Leon, Nedra, Anita, Rolf, Nora, Alice, Carol ...' and ending '... Lora, Cecil, Aaron, Flora, Tina, Arden, Noel and Ellen *sinned*!' Quite an orgy! The other, undoubtedly my favourite, was a little seven-worder which must be dedicated to all those who, like myself, lead curiously disjointed lives because of our unlikely working hours. It runs: 'Naomi, sex at noon taxes, I moan.'

'Uoy ot gninrom doog yrev a.'

We reached the ultimate in all this when I interviewed on the programme the original palindromic woman. She was a German housewife called Katya Nik – whose very name made about as much sense backwards as forwards. She claimed to conduct entire conversations back to front. She said she had acquired the knack as a child, when she and her sister held secret discussions in this way. She not only reversed the order of the words, she reversed the words themselves.

When she came to the studio, however, it seemed that she was not at her best in the early morning. Having first suggested that she had a go at reversing a ten-minute news bulletin, then a two-minute news summary, and finally just the headlines, all without any success, we eventually settled for my standard 'Today' greeting. That meant she had to say 'Uoy ot gninrom doog yrev a.' And so she did, without hesitation. I laboriously wrote it out, as you see it here, and tried to say it also. We recorded both our efforts, then played the tape backwards. My own version was completely unintelligible, but full marks to Mrs Nik. She came through perfectly clearly: 'A very good morning to you!'

5 Where Our Caravan Has Rested

Mostly it has rested at party conferences. These gatherings attract almost as many media folk as delegates. Indeed, papers like The Guardian *frequently delight in totting up the total BBC attendance and unkindly suggest that if we had a block vote, we could probably decide party policy for the next year. They forget to mention that while* The Guardian *has to meet only one deadline and fill only one issue each day – not necessarily with the same day's news – the BBC has deadlines all round the clock, filling a vast assortment of news and current affairs pro-grammes on two television networks, four domestic radio services, all the local radio stations and the World Service. Thus there is no little activity where our caravan has rested during these conferences and, not surprisingly, problems can occur.*

The caravan is a mobile studio, normally parked alongside the conference hall. The only conference venue where it is not required is Blackpool, where a temporary studio is set up in the basement of the Imperial Hotel, the conference headquarters. This has the advantage of allowing Cabinet ministers to be interviewed in their dressing gowns and carpet slippers. The snag is that a basement is still a basement, even when it is a studio, and by the end of the week one longs for the sight of the outside world and a breath of fresh air.

The caravan, on the other hand, offers a maximum of both. A new vehicle introduced in 1982 possesses a magnificent picture window, which at Yarmouth with the SDP afforded me a panoramic view throughout the programme of the sun coming up over Yarmouth beach, early-morning risers walking their dogs along the seashore and fishing boats coming into harbour. It made it difficult to concentrate on the intricacies of industrial strategy and statutory incomes policies. As for fresh air, at Bournemouth with the Liberals it was so powerful that the caravan rocked precariously throughout the morning, which caused David Steel to enquire nervously whether we were actually being blown out to sea.

But the greatest hazard we have faced in the 'mobile' is Mr Cyril Smith. I am sure he will not mind me saying it, since happily he is not bashful about his size; when Mr Steel made a publicity record set to music, Mr Smith observed, 'If David goes into pop music, I'm going into belly-dancing!'

In our original caravan, extra jacks were put underneath to ensure that it did not tip on end as he moved along it. The new model was made of firmer stuff, but the designers had still provided only a narrow doorway into the studio itself. This nearly beat Mr Smith (he has the same trouble, he told us, getting into British Rail lavatories), and he was still struggling to get through it one morning as the moment approached for our live interview. He just made it, but not before I visualised myself announcing, 'I have just been joined in the studio by the top half of Cyril Smith!'

Most of the leading politicians of the day have passed through that caravan in the early morning. Indeed, at one moment during the 1982 Conservative conference we had four Cabinet ministers in it simultaneously. It occurred to me that if Carlos or any of his terrorist mates had hitched us up and towed us away, it could have created quite a gap at Westminster.

'I have just been joined in the studio by the top half of Cyril Smith!'

Only Mrs Thatcher has consistently declined to be interviewed on 'Today' at a party conference, at any rate since she became Prime Minister. I fear I may have been responsible, for in her last year as Leader of the Opposition I did interview her during the conference. We shared a sofa in the intimacy of her suite, but unfortunately I had the most appalling cold. I could only emerge from my handkerchief for brief moments to gasp out the next clogged-up question. She was extremely sympathetic, but a little later she was sneezing her head off in the conference hall. She has declined our invitation at party conferences ever since.

Broadcasts from party conferences, like any other outside broadcasts, are subject to technical hazards. Producers' voices are liable to break into the programme, exhorting interviewers to cut short their discussions, exchanging unpleasantries with their opposite numbers in London, and on one memorable occasion complaining to the nation that the damned review of the papers had over-run. Broadcasters themselves tend to be wary of micro-phones, just in case they are 'live', but I dropped my guard during the 1979 Liberal assembly in Margate, the town which has never recovered from Clement Freud's observa-tion to the conference, having been billeted in a Butlin-owned hotel, that he had been appointed chairman of the hotel escape committee.

I was interviewing Mr Freud on this topic – one of the few lively ones at the conference, as I recall – when I was instructed on my headphones to cut the interview short before we had reached the main point. Dutifully, but fuming, I did so. Hugh Sykes, presenting from London, started to introduce the next item and, assuming that only the producer could now hear me, I cried out in frustration, 'You shouldn't have cut me off like that!' Alas, I was heard by millions, including a newspaper columnist who kindly recounted the whole affair in print, expressing the hope that Hugh and I were not kicking each other after our 'fraught exchange', as he called it. Actually, the only person I kicked over that was myself.

The SDP 'rolling conferences' introduced a new peripatetic element into conference coverage, with the 'Today' team travelling on the conference train amid MPs and their supporters, political correspondents, packed plastic dinners and half-bottles of questionable claret. The erstwhile Gang of Four distributed themselves among the compartments, holding impromptu press conferences, preparing their next speeches and trying not to look too overwhelmed by the claret.

The 1982 excursion was marred by an engine failure as we wended our unlikely way across country from Derby to Yarmouth. Anyone who tries to travel by rail from Derby to Yarmouth deserves all he gets, and we were hardly surprised when we came to a halt for an hour and a half in open fenland somewhere between Peterborough and March. Eventually the guard advised us that we would be getting a new engine in March. 'Great heavens,' I heard myself cry despairingly, 'and this is only October.' During the delay, with almost an entire political party held hostage by British Rail, community singing broke out in one compartment – 'If you were the only Shirl in the world, and I were the only Roy' – a cut-throat card school got under way in another, the claret ran out in all of them, and Mr Roy Jenkins, who had previously declined to be interviewed, finally succumbed to my tape recorder just to pass the time.

This sort of thing is only a minor frustration compared with trying to make a compelling programme out of a party

47

conference, of whatever colour. My first extra-mural activity after spending a week at one of them was to conduct a quiz for young business managers. I was able to tell them what a relief it was, after a week of interviewing politicians, to ask a question and have some reasonable expectation of actually getting an answer!

6 It Seemed A Good Idea At The Time

The eccentric inventor can always be sure of a couple of minutes on 'Today'. Over the years we have cherished the gardener who grew square tomatoes, the mechanic who ran his car on chicken manure, the considerate husband who invented a noiseless alarm clock (it vibrated underneath his pillow). Some have gone on to greater glory, others have sunk without trace. Either way, they have enlivened our early mornings and so have earned our admiration and our gratitude.

Anyone with an antidote for some fairly universal but rarely fatal complaint receives a sympathetic hearing on 'Today'. We are more cautious with the man who has a cure for cancer or can eliminate arthritis or has a palliative for Parkinson's disease. It is not our business to raise false hopes and the repercussions can be heart-breaking if we unwittingly publicise a medical charlatan or idiot. But where the efforts are genuine, where some tangible results can be quoted and where no great harm is done if it is all proved wrong, then let us not scorn the man with the new benefit for mankind, no matter how unlikely it may be.

Hay fever, which lays so many of us low during the summer months, is the sort of complaint which encourages such ingenuity. In our time we have come across the 'Angel Water' which gushes up under the car park of a pub in Essex. It provides nourishment for a neighbouring watercress bed but is also sold by the publican to hay fever sufferers for bathing the eyes and the nose, for drinking, and indeed for standing in if acquired in sufficient quantity.

There is the mechanical air purifier, a modern development of the traditional moist cloth on the window sill, which is said to trap the pollen as it enters the room. If that fails there is the final line of defence, a smear of vaseline under the nostrils to intercept the pollen at the point of entry. Once past that, it can still be countered, so contributors to the programme have told us, by honey or garlic pills or cider vinegar.

Much more spectacular, and a great talking point on 'Today' in its time, was the Hincherton Hay Fever Helmet, a device like an inverted plastic goldfish bowl into which pure air was pumped through a filter; it was powered by a hair-dryer engine and six rechargeable batteries all attached to the wearer's belt. Mr Richard Hinchcliffe of Pershore in Worcestershire explained to us how he drove to work in Birmingham each morning in the hay fever season wearing this contraption, to the consternation of his fellow commuters. The helmet was so capacious it could accommodate the most elaborate hairstyle or even a medium-sized hat.

'It is worth being stared at,' he told us, 'just to stop the streaming nose and the gummed-up eyes and the everlasting sneezing. All I know is, it works. It is my own portable controlled environment.' It was particularly useful, he added, while cutting the lawn.

Snoring is a less distressing complaint, and indeed for the snorer it is not distressing at all, but it is a frequent threat to marital bliss and has thus attracted many ingenious attempts at curing it. We did not take too seriously the suggestion by a Mr Hayward of North London of a nose hose, which fitted over the mouth and enabled the sleeping snorer to blow automatically into his own ear. It could be fitted with a scent pellet that encouraged the snorer to sniff, thus further

'... a device like an inverted plastic goldfish bowl ...'

reducing the snoring, or it could be tuned like a Tibetan flute to produce a soothing warble. But somehow it seemed unlikely to catch on.

We were also sceptical about the idea of a Dr Raymond Rosen of New Jersey for a machine which recorded the level of the snores and woke up the snorer by setting off an alarm when the noise got too appalling. Nor did we take to the solution devised by a Los Angeles neurologist, Dr J. Dewitt Fox – a contoured collar which was originally produced to treat headaches and neck pains but was also found to prevent snoring. Even his suggestion of a luxury version with mink and rhinestones to wear to the opera failed to tempt us.

A more serious suggestion, and one which actually led to an interview, came from a French scientist called Dr Pierre Gros. His theory was that if the nasal passages are dry, the air that is breathed in through the nose tends to vibrate, thus producing the snore. Central heating, smoking and alcohol all tend to intensify the drying-out process. Dr Gros therefore devised a spray which had to be squirted into each nostril before retiring. It was supposed to keep the nasal passages moist and consequently silent for up to eight hours. He compared the effect to the noise made by wet tissue paper as against the noise if it is dry.

His spray was actually marketed in Britain at £1.75 a bottle, enough to last the snorer for up to six weeks. On the other hand, as we suggested at the time, a prod in the back could be applied for nothing.

❖   ❖   ❖

The ultimate in medical inventions, as far as the 'Today' programme was prepared to go, was the nasal contraceptive. Not unnaturally, we exercise a certain caution on these matters since not everybody wishes to be reminded at breakfast time of what they were probably thinking about quite a lot the night before. This device, however, seemed novel enough to warrant a few minutes on the latter half of the programme after the teenagers had gone to school (as they probably knew all about it already). We hoped it would not embarrass too much those people who normally used inhalers to suppress a sneeze or a snuffle and would never dare to do so again.

It so happened that on that same morning I spotted another fascinating nasal link with the reproductive process. It was reported that American scientists (it is always 'American scientists') had deduced that the heavy breathing one normally associates with this activity is not due just to deep passion, or even to a basic shortage of breath. It is because the erectile membranes in the nose, as in the case of erectile membranes elsewhere about the person, are inclined to expand on such occasions. Elsewhere about the person this is jolly useful, not to say essential. Inside the nose it merely congests the nasal passages and gives rise to the noisy panting so beloved of the cinema director and the romantic novelist. It was even suggested that love at first sight might well be revealed by the blocking of the nostrils, a theory which must cause frightful complications during the hay fever season.

But back to the nasal contraceptive. British scientists (and how much more convincing that sounds than 'American scientists') had developed a nasal spray which, if inhaled twice a day, was supposed to have the same contraceptive effect as the Pill, without any of the undesirable side effects. It was an idea, we did not hesitate to point out, not to be sniffed at. If only it could be combined with the anti-snore spray, the nation could really sleep peacefully in its beds.

◈ ◈ ◈

Among the inventions which came our way with less obvious benefits to mankind was Sandy McAngus's Levatarium. Judging by its name, this had all the makings of a great April Fool, but Sandy McAngus really did exist. He was a second-year student at Edinburgh University and he had spent fifteen months perfecting a vertical wind tunnel so powerful that a man could fly in the airflow.

Why any man should want to do this was not too clear. Mr McAngus talked bravely about its uses for training combat soldiers, who would presumably find it necessary from time to time to make a vertical take-off, Harrier-style, to the confusion of their enemies. Remembering that famous photograph of Marilyn Monroe on the hot-air grating with her skirt around her ears, I think a better bet would have been to flog the gadget around the fairgrounds, where one could see the potential of a device which propelled the paying customers upwards.

The story was mainly worth reporting in order to introduce this delightful new word into the nation's vocabulary. Could a levatarium also be described as a wind closet, I pondered – only to be reprimanded by Brian for showing too much (ho ho) levity.

We were assured that a company had been set up to market this thing, and patent rights taken out. Alas, I cannot recall ever having heard of Sandy McAngus again. Perhaps he disappeared up his own levatarium.

It is never wise, however, to joke about inventions. The next generation may well take them for granted and just joke about us for our innocence. We learned this lesson very thoroughly from an aeronautical expert who came in to discuss what looked like ludicrous designs for the aeroplanes of the future.

How about, for instance, the Ring Wing airliner, which looked like any other airliner except that the wings curled round and met over the top of the fuselage? Or the Delta Wing Spanloader, which had no fuselage at all – it was just a monstrous wing with a tail at each end and six engines hanging underneath. Then there was the Dual Fuselage, a sort of aerial catamaran with two fuselages sharing the same wing; the Logistics Transport, which combined flying with hovering and wafted across the sea at 300 mph with a payload of 200 tons; and the Large Sea Loiter Amphibian, which could fly for 4000 miles and 'sit down' for ten hours at a time in waves of up to twenty feet.

Dotty? The Advanced Concepts Department at Lockeed-Georgia, which dreamed them up, did not think so. Nor did our aeronautical expert. After all, he pointed out, who would have visualised a few years ago that a plane could take off as vertically as a helicopter? Or that a plane could fly into space on the back of a rocket? A hundred years ago, who would have believed a plane would fly at all?

We started that interview as a bit of a chuckle. When we finished it, we were not sure who was laughing at whom.

There are some inventions, though, which even the inventors can hardly take seriously – even if they may prove quite profitable until the joke wears off. For example there was the man in Miami who invented subliminal notepaper. It was based on the same principle, he assured us, as subliminal advertising. Just as messages can be conveyed in television commercials without the viewer consciously seeing them, why not impregnate notepaper so it can influence the reader without actually being noticed? It could bring a whole new dimension to letter-writing. I remember commenting that not even stationery can stand still.

He had special notepaper, for instance, for job applications. It subliminally conveyed what a splendid chap the applicant was. Similarly, a letter of criticism or complaint could be given an extra subliminal punch, while an apparently innocuous love-letter could convey all manner of subliminal erotica.

The way he did it was of course a secret. It was so secret that scientists who examined the paper could find nothing unusual about it at all. But he must have conveyed some sort of subliminal message to the letter-writing public. because the paper was selling briskly at the equivalent of 50p a sheet.

The interview produced its own crop of correspondence, because it included the comment that the investigating scientists 'drew a complete blank'. In the context of subliminal notepaper, it occurred to me to ask how a complete blank could be physically drawn. Forthwith some of our more solid listeners, out in the shires, wrote in to explain (what in fact as an ex-Norfolk resident I knew well enough already) that 'drawing' was used in the locomotional rather than the artistic sense, and it was all to do with looking for foxes in coverts. The subliminal message in these letters came through clearly enough: this man is an urban idiot. Only one listener got the point, and he sensibly suggested that to draw a blank you needed (ho ho) invisible ink.

7 'Dear "Today" Programme, Is This A Record?'

Alas, it very rarely is, but that does not stop people from trying. Generally it is some sort of lunacy being perpetrated in the sacred name of sponsorship, to raise money for charity. I have often observed plaintively that all the energy expanded on marathon darts matches, or paddling bedsteads across the Channel, or running backwards round Regents Park, should really be put to much more productive use – like digging my garden. So far I have failed to convince anyone.

The sort of achievement which is likely to get you a couple of minutes on 'Today' will probably not qualify for the *Guinness Book of Records*. It is generally too daft even for that. For instance, the book may well record the fastest ascent of Mount Kilimanjaro, but would it bother to note the progress of two army sergeants who set out to climb that same mountain three-legged?

We interviewed them before they started, their nearside legs duly lashed together, and I remember musing that if they left tracks in the snow it could start a whole new legend about three-legged Yetis. Oddly enough, I can find no record of us ever talking to them again. Perhaps the climb is taking longer than they thought.

❖ ❖ ❖

The exploit which provoked the most lively speculation was that of an Essex vicar, the Rev. Timothy Thompson, who decided to sit on his church roof for a week, equipped with a loud-hailer to harangue passers-by, a basket on a rope for drawing up supplies, and a telephone, kindly loaned by Buzby. The idea was to raise money for his church repair fund, presumably before it collapsed underneath him.

We phoned him a couple of times on the programme, and I ventured to put a question which fascinated all my colleagues in the 'Today' team: up there on his lofty and very exposed perch, how did he answer the calls of Nature? The Rev. Timothy informed me that in his native New Zealand he had learned from the Maoris their ancient skill of containing themselves for long periods. He was therefore suffering no embarrassment or discomfort.

We were still digesting this information when a letter arrived from a Mr Fletcher of Lower Heswell in the Wirral. The vicar, he said, had cleared up a long-standing mystery. 'Have you noticed those extraordinary facial expressions and dances performed by Maori warriors and New Zealand rugby players? We were always led to believe they were a form of war dance. Obviously this is nonsense. Having been bottled up for a week, they are merely asking to be pointed to the nearest loo.'

The Vicar himself had the last word. He was unable to divulge any further details, he said, but as soon as he came down from that roof he would be harvesting his spaghetti crop! We shall no doubt be hearing from him again, next April the First.

'Today' became quite deeply involved in what must be the longest-ever sponsored walk. It was known officially as the Trans-Globe Expedition, and it went on for years. You will recall that Sir Ranulph Fiennes and Charles Burton visited both the North and the South Poles en route, and our link

'... he had learned from the Maoris their ancient skill of
containing themselves for long periods.'

with them during the trickiest sections was Sir Ranulph's remarkable wife, Virginia, who manned the radio-telephone at their base camp. During the final stages, as they headed across the Arctic, we were in almost daily contact with her on the programme.

We were the first to receive her personal accounts of the fire which destroyed their reserve equipment, the damage to one of the supply planes which left them dangerously short of food, the disappearance through the ice of Sir Ranulph's snowmobile (he was on it at the time), and various other hazards which must have added zest to countless breakfast tables.

Our conversations were made more dramatic by the variable quality of our radio-telephone link with the Arctic Circle. The realism of a long-distance link-up can be destroyed by its embarrassing clarity: we can often get better quality from Sydney than from Surbiton, and listeners suspect that we are rigging the whole thing inside the studio. In those conversations with Lady Fiennes, though, you could almost hear the wind howling, the snow beating on the tents and the huskies yelping outside. It got so bad sometimes that I had to act as interpreter, repeating Lady F's answers as well as my questions and occasionally only guessing at what she said. All this seemed to paint the picture more graphically, and as the tale unfolded each morning I could visualise the listeners getting more and more involved – Dad with icicles on his beard trudging off through the blizzard to make contact with the 8.12 supply ship to Waterloo, Mum cutting strips of seal-meat and blubber for the children's sandwiches.

I have yet to meet the Fiennes, though I gather that Sir Ranulph and I frequently follow in each other's tracks these days – not across the Arctic but around the luncheon clubs. We did interview Charles Burton and his delightful wife soon after they had been reunited after months of separation. My abiding impression was that while it was an amazing achievement to complete that epic journey, with someone as attractive as Mrs Burton around, it was an amazing achievement ever to start out on it.

From the longest walk to the longest word. Nothing to do with sponsorship, just straightforward curiosity. I had always believed that 'anti-disestablishmentarianism' with 28 letters was the longest word in the English language. One morning I was foolish enough to say so. I was soon put right.

An American psychologist attending a conference in Edinburgh was the first on the phone. He offered a 29-letter word to beat it: 'anti-deinstitutionalizationism.' He assured us he had not just made it up. He defined it as 'a movement which is against the policy of moving long-term psychiatric patients out into the community', and I was in no position to argue.

That was soon overtaken by another American product, a medical term which came into the news after the eruption of the Mount St Helen's volcano. It produced an exceptionally fine dust which caused an irritation in the lungs technically known as pneumonoultramicroscopic-silicovolcanonconitosis. That is 47 letters and, according to our informant, it was officially recognised in American dictionaries as the longest English word.

For once we could beat the Americans at their own sort of eccentric record. Once you are into medical or technical terms not even the end of the page is the limit. Mr Peter Pearce, whose firm happens to supply the BBC's stationery, used up several pages of his own to quote from *Mrs Byrnes' Dictionary of Unusual, Obscure and Preposterous Words*, which bristled with what he called hippopotomonstrosesquipedalian words – and that wasn't bad for a start.

The briefest was a mere 47 letters, a kind of acid called aqueosalinocalinocetaceoaluminosocuprevitriolic. A translation of Aristophanes' word for a special kind of goulash, which ran to 170 letters in the original Greek, took on an extra dozen in the English version. For the sake of the typesetter's sanity, let us not actually reproduce it – doubters can always consult Mrs Byrnes. Certainly it is not worth devoting a couple of pages to her longest offering, a 1913-letter monstrosity said to be the chemical name for some sort of protein containing 267 amino acids. It starts with 'methionyl ...' and ends with '... arginylserine' and has 60-odd lines of similar gibberish in between.

As a bonus, Mr Pearce also quoted the rather charming Indian name for a certain lake in Massachusetts, which I actually managed to say one morning without getting too mixed up between the 'goggags' and the 'bunagungs'. The complete word is Chargoggagoggmanchauggagoggchaubunagungamaugg, which is a lot more fun than that interminable Welsh railway station. The meaning is rather fun too: 'You fish on your side, I fish on my side, nobody fish in the middle.' The EEC fishery ministers could do a lot worse.

◈ ◈ ◈

The official all-time record for English words is held by another protein which has 8000 letters. Under the ho-ho rules of 'Today', however, we could still beat that. One listener, probably an avid reader of the *Beano*, claimed the record should go to 'smiles', because there was a mile between the first and last letters. Then came the suggestion 'beleaguered', because by the same reasoning that was three times as long. But the 'Today' award finally went to words like 'taut' and 'laud' because, as Mr Alan Schramm of Ilford pointed out, the 'AU' stands for 'Astronomical Unit', and that is approximately 93,000,000 miles long!

While on the subject of record words, we were once challenged to find a longer single palindromic word than 'deified'. Anything like 'toot-toot' or 'pip-pip' was not allowed. So far, 'deified' still holds the 'Today' record.

Every year or so, a listener's letter sparks off another search for the aptest surname. It is a regular feature of the newspaper gossip columns, always useful for filling an odd three lines, and we use it in the same way to fill the spare thirty seconds.

Everyone must have a personal favourite, whether it be the Norwich chief sanitary engineer of the 1950s whose name adorned all the city's dustcarts, W.C. Smelley; or the piano-tuner in Whalley called F. Sharp; or the dentist I heard about in Bristol called Fillingham (or another in Hammersmith called Phang). Combinations of names are popular too. An Epsom listener told me about a chemist's shop which bore the names of Philpotts and Spillam, and one of our many listeners in the Irish Republic took the trouble to send a local telephone directory which contained the Sligo solicitors' firm of Argue and Phibbs.

Many of our Norfolk listeners reminded us of the Gotobed family of Great Snoring, and Mr C. G. Keightley of Boston in Lincolnshire recalled that the man who used to live at the gatehouse to the local cemetery was called Mr Gabriel.

The memory of Mr Charles Davis of Helston in Cornwall went back even further. When he was at school sixty-five years earlier, he recalled, there was always a giggle during the alphabetical roll-call when the headmaster called out 'Fairweather' followed by 'Fowle'. And another schoolboy memory was of a lad called Parts who caused great delight when he joined the cadet force and became Pte. Parts.

It became apparent from our correspondence that British Telecom employ a remarkable number of people called

Busby. We also heard of the cashier at a Dorset bank called Miss Open, whose nameplate on the counter had I. B. OPEN on one side and of course TILL CLOSED on the other. Among the newspaper cuttings of court cases involving apt names, perhaps the best involved a man called Pigeon who was caught inside a club by a security guard called Peacock and arrested by a detective constable called Bird. He is not actually 'doing bird' – he pleaded guilty and received a fine.

Perhaps my favourite, though, appeared in another newspaper report about an Iranian terrorist who was badly injured when his bomb blew up in his own car. His name was Fooladi.

A variation on the apt surname cropped up during the Falklands war. The name of the air force member of Argentina's ruling junta at that time was sometimes spelt, and certainly pronounced, Lamedoso. A number of people pointed out that this was made up of four notes in the tonic solfa – La Me Do So. But when the Argentines had surrendered and the junta had disappeared in different directions, Mrs I. Tindale of Gateshead made the excellent point that Lamedoso spelt backwards is 'O sod 'em al'!

During each Christmas season we have tried without success to pinpoint the first appearance of Christmas cards in the shops. We suspect that in some shops they never bother to pack them away. We have however received some remarkable claims for the earliest and fastest card to be delivered.

It started with a listener mentioning she had had a card from Zimbabwe marked 'Surface Mail' which had taken only three days to reach her, early in November. Miss Sandy Bennett of York said that she too had had a three-day delivery by 'Surface Mail' from Zimbabwe early in October – yet a letter from Zimbabwe marked 'Air Mail' had taken fifteen days. For anyone sending letters from Zimbabwe, the moral is obvious.

The record must go to Mrs Mary Whine of Feltham in Middlesex. She sent me an envelope posted in Sydney, New South Wales, on 26 October which actually reached her on 27 October. It no doubt had something to do with crossing the International Date Line, but even so it was a remarkable postal feat.

Meanwhile, as many listeners reminded us, first-class mail inside the UK could still take three days and second-class mail anything up to a week. Only when the Post Office is presented with some sort of challenge does it seem to excel. There are many records claimed for obscurely-addressed letters being safely delivered. I remember the writer Iris Bryce, who lives on a canal boat, telling me that mail addressed to the boat was sometimes dropped into her lap by a postman leaning over a bridge as she chugged underneath it. Typical of the sorters' ingenuity was to track down 'The woman upstairs in the antique market by the river and a bridge leading from the short-stay-long-stay centre car park in Salisbury, Wilts' – particularly as it was spelt 'Sailsbury'. No postcode-conscious computer could have solved that!

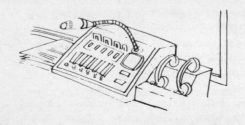

8 April The First — A Rather Special Day On 'Today'

It is rather special to me because on April the First 1970 I joined the 'Today' programme as a full-time presenter, which must make me the longest-running April Fool victim in history. But ever since Richard Dimbleby presented his classic report on the spaghetti forests of central Italy, the BBC has had a special affection for April Fool's Day stories, and what programme is better fitted to report them than 'Today'?

The exploits of Major John Blashford-Snell, explorer extraordinary, have been regularly reported on 'Today'. Wherever there is an uncharted river to be charted, an impenetrable forest to be penetrated, a trackless desert to be tracked, 'Blashers' is there. He has been involved in underwater archaeology in the Mediterranean, treks across the Sahara, the first crossing by motor vehicle of the Darien Gap in Panama and Colombia and, most dramatic of all, the 3000-mile journey from the source to the mouth of the Congo River, now known as the Zaire. In the tradition of Captain Kirk and Mr Spock, 'Blashers' has boldly gone where no man has gone before.

All of this lent enormous weight to the interview he gave me one April morning in 1975, just after he had returned from his Zaire expedition. He came into the studio to disclose, exclusively to the 'Today' programme, how he had explored a tributary of that mighty river, known locally as the Zampopo, and had discovered a long-lost tribe which still worshipped the sacred pith helmet of Sanders of the River.

The helmet had a particular significance for the tribe, since their own heads were lower than their shoulders because of generations of heavy load-carrying. Thus they could not wear any headgear themselves and they marvelled greatly at those who could. Their chief was the only one who had experienced the joys of civilisation. He led the sacred chant, 'Goingup goingup goingup', to which his followers replied, 'Goingdown goingdown goingdown'. This apparently originated from his experiences as a lift-man at the Dorchester Hotel.

As for the sacred pith helmet, Major Blashford-Snell brought an exact replica to the studio, and I have it still as a reminder of that remarkable expedition. We treated it with proper respect, exchanging the traditional greeting of the Zampopo tribe, 'Pith off'. I also still treasure a copy of his book about the Zaire expedition, *In the Steps of Stanley* (should it not have more correctly been *In the Wake of Stanley?*) inscribed 'To John Timpson – a souvenir of the Great Zampopo Expedition – from John Blashford-Snell of the River.'

These days 'Blashers' occupies himself with more mundane pursuits. He is in charge of the Army training scheme for young unemployed and doubtless imbues them with the same urge to seek out the inaccessible – like jobs. But even while confined to the British Isles, his spirit of adventure remains uncurbed. The last I heard of him, he was hunting the Loch Ness Monster – in an airship!

That Zampopo interview was in 1975. On the same April morning we carried the dramatic report of a bird-lover who was planning to tow an island in the Medway out of the path of shipping, to preserve the nesting-place of the rare black-

67

'... planning to tow an island in the Medway out of the path of shipping ...'

headed gull. We also passed on a warning from our man in Dover that the white cliffs were being attacked by some virulent form of verdigris and were actually turning green. It was a memorable morning.

April Fool's Day 1982 brought its usual crop of tall stories. The Swiss Government, we reported, was protesting about British cake manufacturers using the term 'Swiss roll'. The reporter involved was called Sam Jaffa, which made it sound even more far-fetched. Actually it was quite true, and the story prompted many ingenious listeners to suggest alternative names.

The most popular was 'swish roll', not just because it sounded posher or slightly alcoholic, but because the original name was said to come from having to whisk or swish the eggs to make the roll. One lady wrote, 'If the Swiss think our Swiss roll is a swizzle, let us call it a swizz roll.' Another liked the term used by a small boy, 'wound-up cake', and in the same mould came the idea of a spiroll.

Other correspondents were much more interested in the implications of the Swiss protest. If it is upheld, said Pauline Bacon (her real name), what shall we have to call Brussels sprouts, Viennese whirls, Danish pastries and Milanaise sauce? Indeed, I thought, it might be an improvement if Scotch eggs had to be 70 per cent proof. Joan Howes of Basingstoke summed it all up in a verse she called 'Oh Crumbs!':

> The Swiss, it seems, are taking us to court
> For misdemeanour of a trifling sort.
> A common cake that always bore their name
> Becomes a pawn within the racist game.
> What scenes might follow if they should succeed
> In their indictment of this harmless deed?
> Will Battenburgs start tearing out their hair

69

In protest at an almond-pasted square?
African tarts could rapidly incite
Chaste tribal beauties to assert their right
To change the name of such confectionery
As might impute their impropriety.
The men of Eccles in a sterling band
Might equally protest throughout the land
That currant-cushioned pastries could bear blame
For casting some aspersion on their name.
As yet the belles of Holland find their hearts
Unbroken by the name Dutch apple tarts,
But Moscow could turn nasty in a trice
Each time we bite into a Russian slice.
The pitfalls could be endless. Every day
We masticate our status quo away,
Munching the path to international strife,
While brandishing a two-edged pastry knife!

On that same morning, April the First 1982, we carried an even less believable story. It was the one about Britain sending a nuclear submarine to deal with ten Argentine scrap merchants who had landed on South Georgia. Alas, that was true, too.

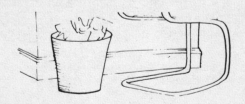

9 The Eccentrics —
Life-Blood Of 'Today'

*'The world considers eccentricity in great
things, genius; in small things, folly,' said Bulwer
Lytton in one of his off-moments. 'Today'
considers eccentricity in anybody a most
welcome relief. It offers a respite from pontifica-
ting politicians, erudite economists, ubiquitous
union leaders. When the famous names on a
programme have dissolved into a blur of
unemployment figures and interest rates and
common agricultural policies, the eccentric
shines on, a reminder that in this stereotyped
world there is still a place for the individual.
Some of them may merit little more than their
cue. What more does one need to know, for
instance, about a clairvoyant chip-shop owner
in Wigan who guessed what a customer would
order from the colour of his car? Or the
Doncaster businessman who went to work in a
mechanical digger because he was fed up with
having his Rolls Royce vandalised? But others
deserve closer scrutiny: 'men of uncommon
abilities', as Goethe put it (on the same page of
my dictionary of quotations as Bulwer Lytton),
'who fall into eccentricities when their sphere of
life is not adequate to their powers.'*

Baron Gore-Booth of Maltby, GCMG, KCVO, former head
of Her Majesty's Diplomatic Service, has a most distinguished record as a diplomat and a civil servant. His entry in

71

Who's Who contains an imposing list of the offices he has held, from High Commissioner in India to Registrar of the Order of St Michael and St George. He started at Eton and Balliol, progressed through the Foreign Service and ended with a directorship of Grindlays Bank – an impeccable pedigree. He wrote an autobiography called *With Great Truth and Respect*, and edited an edition of *Satow's Guide to Diplomatic Practice*.

It is only when you come to the last line of the entry that a less orthodox note is struck. His clubs are listed as the Athenaeum, which is to be expected, and the Baker Street Irregulars, which is not. But Lord Gore-Booth is indeed a past president and still an enthusiastic member of the Sherlock Holmes Society of London.

This is not just a passing foible. When I first met him he was off to the Reichenbach Falls in Switzerland to re-enact the dramatic final encounter between Holmes and the 'Napoleon of Crime', Professor Moriarty. His party all travelled in full Victorian dress, to the astonishment of their fellow package-tourists, and Lord Gore-Booth himself arrived in the 'Today' studio that morning in full Holmesian regalia of Inverness cape and deerstalker hat. Mercifully, he did refrain from puffing on his meerschaum before breakfast.

He told us that he first read Conan Doyle's stories as a boy, then returned to them at the Foreign Office, presumably during the tea-breaks, and had been devoted to the 'sacred writings' ever since. In his view there was a certain similarity between the diplomat and the detective – they both had to be self-reliant and independent. His favourite tale, I recall, was 'The Speckled Band'. His favourite character was of course Holmes himself, though he was much fascinated by the matrimonial affairs of the good Dr Watson, who was thought to have married twice or even three times, but because of various inconsistencies in the stories it was not clear when or where or to whom. The last I heard, Lord Gore-Booth was still trying to sort this out.

I am sure that in the tradition of his hero, he will not permit such a mystery to remain unsolved.

Not only the Sherlock Holmes Society enjoys re-enacting the past in appropriate costume. Twentieth-century Cavaliers and Roundheads are thumping each other regularly all over the country, and Morris dancers consider it perfectly normal to put on bells and ribbons and straw hats, and wave staves about in an early version of 'Come Dancing'. Occasionally, however, an individual costumed eccentric emerges to enliven our mundane lives. One such was Mr Edward Prosser, a 38-year-old interior designer from Glamorgan and part-time Welsh dragon.

Mr Prosser made a flying visit to Twickenham in his dragon outfit to cheer on his compatriots in the England–Wales match of 1982. Alas, his enthusiasm overcame him, as it has so many Rugby fans. Unlike Miss Erica Roe, another Twickenham enthusiast, he did not finish up topless and famous: he finished up legless and famous. He made a spectacular appearance in court next morning, complete with his wings, his long tail and his massive mouthful of gold teeth. It was explained that he had nothing else to wear. In spite of his protests that he was animal, not human, and a personal pet of the Prince of Wales to boot, he was fined £10 for being drunk and disorderly. The court refused to accept his plea that after three bottles of wine and several lagers he would normally, like any other dragon, just let off steam but in this case had been forced to resort to a Welsh leak.

He was still in his costume when he went into his local studio on his return home to explain his remarkable origins. It seems that after some 1500 years down the pit he caught dragoniosis and came to the surface to recover on a diet of lager and nutty slack. He complained bitterly that at the police station he had been fed a breakfast of egg on toast

'He made a spectacular appearance in court next morning ...'

instead of his customary firelighters, but he assured me that he bore the police no grudge for 'dragon' him off to custody. He also denied that he had returned home with his tail between his legs.

Altogether a splendid eccentric who cheered up thousands of Rugby fans, brought some much-appreciated light relief into West London Magistrates Court, and surely raised a smile over many a breakfast table, whether it bore eggs on toast or nutty slack.

Gamblers may well be considered eccentric just because they gamble, but some of the bets they take must remove any lingering doubts. One such which featured on 'Today' was made by an antique dealer at Shoreham in Sussex, Mr Paul Emery, who bet a friend that he would achieve his life's ambition of conducting a symphony concert at the Royal Albert Hall by the time he was 40. We met Mr Emery when he was 39. By then it had become apparent that his talents were not going to be recognised in time to win his bet, so he decided to speed things up a bit by renting the Albert Hall and hiring an orchestra himself. All that remained was to sell 4,300 tickets.

Mr Emery had only done a little amateur conducting in his life, and none at all for the last six years or so. His chances of breaking even therefore seemed pretty thin, since the actual bet was only a matter of a few pounds. Nevertheless we wished him well, and no doubt the orchestra and the proprietors of the Albert Hall are hoping that another will be born in the next minute, too.

The older people get, the more endearingly eccentric some of them become. We enjoyed talking to Mrs Marion

Garbut, the Galloping Granny, star of her local riding school at Burscough in Lancashire. Mrs Garbut was 71 when she decided she wanted to learn how to drive. Unfortunately she could not find an insurance company willing to cover her, so she decided that if she could not travel on four wheels, she would do so on four legs and enrolled at the riding school. After six months she was proficient enough to go on a riding holiday in the Lake District.

Equally game was Miss Elizabeth Forster of Wiveton in Norfolk, whom I met just before she set off on her eighth or ninth trek across the Himalayas. She was 74 at the time and looked twenty years younger. She spurned any form of transport, four-wheeled or four-legged, and walked everywhere in the mountains, up to heights of 18,000 feet. All her treks had been made solo except for the local sherpas, who to her great gratification addressed her as 'Mummy'. Not everyone, she said, could claim to be mother of a nation. On this latest journey she had decided she needed company, so she was taking a woman companion with her – aged 78!

The secret of her stamina, I think, was her life in Norfolk, where the weather can offer anything as unpleasant as the Himalayas, and her twenty-six years in the BBC, which had doubtless prepared her for all manner of unexpected adversities. When she was not on her travels she was writing about them, and during her non-trekking days in Norfolk she divided her time between bird-watching and designing knitting patterns. I have not seen her since that interview, but I suspect she may well live for ever.

There are many collectors in the 'Today' files verging on the eccentric, from the man who collected so many old newspapers that his floor gave way, to the gourmet who collected spiders – and ate them. I suppose the accolade of

Super-Collector must go to Mr Cecil Williamson, who collected collections.

He had a collection of witchcraft and black magic, a collection of smuggling memorabilia, a collection of shells, and various others stored in warehouses and cellars all over the country. In the summer of 1982 he decided to sell some of them off, lock, stock and skeleton – that was in his witchcraft collection. He lived above one of his collections in the gatehouse of Buckfast Abbey in Devon, but the witchcraft museum was at Boscastle in Cornwall and the auctioneers valued the building and its contents at about £200,000. We never heard what it actually raised, but it was no doubt enough to start Mr Williamson on another collection – of nest-eggs.

America at times seems to be almost entirely peopled by eccentrics, judging by the American correspondents of our national Press, and quite a few have been featured on 'Today'. For a number of Christmases, for instance, we followed the fortunes of Roy Collette's moleskin trousers.

Mr Collette and his brother-in-law, Larry Kunkle, sent the trousers to each other every Christmas. The trick was to unpack them in time for the next Christmas. One year Roy welded the trousers inside a 600-pound safe bound with reinforced steel bars. Larry extracted them in time to return them next year in the glove-box of a car which had been crushed into a three-foot cube. Roy got them out with the help of a carbide saw, a blow-torch, an air chisel and a lot of blood, sweat and tears. The last we heard, the trousers had arrived back at Larry's, stuffed inside a six-foot high-abrasion tyre which had also been filled with three tons of concrete.

The whole procedure is so utterly pointless, it may well catch on.

America also produced a great anti-eccentric for the programme, Mr Joseph Troys of Colorado, founder of the International Dull Men's Club and Curator of the Museum of the Ordinary, which mainly features hub-caps and old gardening tools. Mr Troys assured us that he used to be an interesting person but was fortunately rehabilitated. He found it too expensive to keep up with all the trends, his snazzy sports car kept breaking down and he exhausted himself trying to sound sparkling and witty, so he just gave it up. He had occasional lapses when he sounded interesting by accident, but in general he could guarantee to bore the pants off anyone in fifteen minutes.

New members of the Dull Men's Club were usually nominated by loved ones who felt that they had all the qualities of being unutterably dull, but there was also a fairly stiff questionnaire to complete. He did not want members who just pretended to be dull. They were asked, for instance, about their favourite colour; brown or beige were very acceptable but anything like bright red was considered highly questionable. The favourite food ought to be meat loaf or hamburgers, and they would normally wear baggy swimming trunks in public bathing places or saunas.

There was a women's auxiliary, Mr Troys told us, known as the Plain Janes. They had to favour dull men with dull jobs and dull conversations, and they had to be pretty dull themselves. He reckoned about eighty per cent of the American public qualified for membership. What he detested was the 'charismatic over-achiever'; it was the dull people who really kept America going. And from what he had seen of Britain, the same thing applied here too.

If America produces a wide range of eccentrics, Britain can boast one variety peculiar to this country with whom, as a former Male Chauvinist Pig of the Year, I must admit to a certain affinity. It is epitomised by Mr Jeffrey Bernard, described as Low Life Correspondent of *The Spectator* and said to be the only living Englishman who has apologised to the landlord of his local for turning up five minutes later than opening time.

Mr Bernard crossed our path just before Christmas when we were discussing the evils of office parties. The evils, he complained, were not confined to the office. They overflowed into the pubs, and in particular into his pub, which he normally used as an office himself – a place to meet the people he liked, receive messages and occasionally get work.

'Suddenly,' he told us, 'the place is filled with these Christmas idiots. There are the silly little girls who drink Cointreau, then a light ale and a snowball, and round it off with a glass of sherry. They usually end up in tears, being sick, and probably pregnant. With them are the so-called "young executives" with their Mexican moustaches and their aluminium attaché cases filled with copies of *Yachting Monthly* and *Motor Sport*, thinking they've got tremendous style because just once a year they say "Have a drink, and make it a *large* one" – as if there is anything less than a large one.'

Mr Bernard considered there should be the equivalent of 'O' level and 'A' level examinations in drinking, which would have to be passed before admission was permitted to pubs and wine bars. If all this seems a little sour, it should be said that he has probably never recovered since they started serving women in El Vino's. If there is a Gentlemen's Snug left in a British pub which has so far escaped the attentions of the Equal Opportunities Commission, I am sure Mr Bernard would be glad to hear of it. If it refuses to sell Cointreau and snowballs, so much the better.

❖ ❖ ❖

Chrissie Maher is considered an eccentric by many, but an eccentric to whom we all have cause to be grateful. A Liverpudlian in an Eliza Doolittle hat, she has campaigned for years against officialese, gobbledegook and the over-verbose. She started with a market stall at which she offered free advice on how to grapple with incomprehensible official forms. It developed into the Plain English Campaign and is backed by the National Consumer Council which each year presents booby prizes to masters of jargon – one year they received two pounds of tripe, another they got an exquisitely tasteless golden bull. Each year Chrissie comes into the 'Today' studio to tell us about the latest horrors.

This is the sort of thing, an excerpt from the Criminal Justice Act 1982: 'An enactment in which section 31(6) and (7) of the Criminal Law Act 1977 (pre-1949 enactments) produced the same fine or maximum fine for different convictions shall be treated for the purposes of this section as if there were omitted from it so much of it as before 29th July 1977 had the effect that a person guilty of an offence under it was liable on summary conviction to a fine or maximum fine to which he would have been liable if his conviction had satisfied the conditions required for the imposition of the highest fine or maximum fine.'

Or this, a letter from Thorn EMI Domestic Electrical Appliances to people who ordered spare parts: 'Certain of the components comprising our electrical appliances have inherent characteristics the effect of which, whether before or after such components have been introduced into appliances or during such introduction, make it desirable in the interests of safety for the introduction of spare components into, and/or the repair of, our appliances to be carried out by a competent person.'

The Plain English Campaign is not all done for laughs. Chrissie told us how some of this gobbledegook can be positively dangerous, particularly the pidgin-English instructions sometimes issued with foreign-made imported goods. She quoted an Italian do-it-yourself kit for a baby's high chair which included the advice: 'Fix four screws type Z but screw only till half put G in H in the same time with M in L ...' Those screws, said Chrissie, actually supported the chair.

I would not dream of classifying Mrs Mary Whitehouse as a 'Today' eccentric, even though she did once baffle us by awarding us the silver trophy of the National Viewers' and Listeners' Association for our 'sensitivity'. She is inclined, however, to bring out eccentricity in other people, and it was soon after that award in 1981 that I was contacted by the chairman of Titillation in Television, a Mr John Spencer of Ashton-under-Lyne. Here is part of what he wrote on elegantly headed notepaper:

'Titillation in Television has been established because every time one switches on the television these days there is something about sex. Naked women, bedroom scenes, smut and filth everywhere, not to mention homosexuality, innuendo and bad language.

'And quite frankly, there isn't enough of it! There is even less sex on the radio than there is on TV, and it is chaps like you who are largely responsible. Can't you slip in the occasional vulgarity or tasteless joke?

'Is there any chance of a signed photo of Libby Purves in a "provocative" pose? Come to that, is there any chance of a signed photo of yourself in a provocative pose?'

I have preserved the letter beside the citation from Mrs Whitehouse. It serves to keep the award in perspective.

Overseas eccentrics, encountered during our globetrotting days when 'Today' might be presented from Jerusalem during an Israeli General Election, from Detroit during a Republican Convention, from Dublin during the visit of the

81

Pope, or from Peking just because it was Peking, came in a class of their own.

There were the guardsmen, for instance, who paraded each day outside the Parliament Building in Ottawa during the 1981 Western Economic Summit, resplendent in scarlet tunic and bearskins and bayonet-fixed rifles. On closer inspection, half of them turned out to be girl students, earning a few dollars extra during the summer vacation. We Brits thought they were slightly bizarre, but the American tourists loved them.

On that same trip I would have liked to meet the amazing fellow who built the Chateau Montebello, where the Summit was held – proudly claimed to be the biggest log cabin in the world and built entirely of wood. 'Isn't it a fire risk?' I asked, surrounded by thousands and thousands of creosoted logs. 'Don't worry,' said the guide. 'It's fitted with seven thousand sprinklers!'

My favourite overseas eccentric was the pilot of the tiny plane which flew us from Salisbury (now Harare) to Livingstone during our visit to Rhodesia on the last anniversary of UDI before the transfer of power to the new Zimbabwean Government. Those were jumpy days, with white Rhodesians wearing their Armageddon T-shirts – 'Armageddon outa here' – and off-duty white soldiers going a step further with shirts that said 'Join the Rhodesian Army – meet a lot of interesting people – and shoot them.' Our pilot was not quite in this mould, but he carried a tiny revolver stuck in the belt of his shorts and flew his little monoplane as if he was on a strafing run in a Tornado. What made it rather more unreal was his system of navigation, which relied on what looked like an AA map. Fortunately roads are scarce across the Rhodesian bush, and he generally managed to follow the right one.

For his pièce de resistance he suddenly yelled 'Jumbo!', stood the plane on its wing and headed vertically for the ground. We scanned the skies in terror, waiting for a Boeing 747 to cut us in half. It turned out that he had just seen a couple of elephants below us and thought we might like to have a look. A remarkable man; I wonder how he is faring under Mr Mugabe.

Incidentally, while we were at Livingstone we came upon the best anti-litter notice in the ecology business, erected by another eccentric who ran a crocodile farm. He had one enormous specimen, twelve or fifteen feet long and said to be ninety years old, with a long record of dining off the natives. The notice beside his pen said: 'Anyone throwing litter into this pen will be thrown in too'. There was not a toffee-paper in sight.

Perhaps the greatest eccentrics are not the British in Britain, nor foreigners overseas, but Britons abroad. The great days of Empire are over and the pukka sahibs with the stiff upper lips are mostly confined to those old films on television, but the spirit lives on in the occasional far-flung outpost. I found it flourishing in Nicosia, when we were covering the troubles between the Greek and Turkish Cypriots, in the form of a former school-friend of mine, Tony Eggleston. At that time he was headmaster of the English School in Nicosia; he was later to become head of Felsted.

Nicosia was a divided city, with the UN trying inadequately to keep the two sides apart. The tensions often built up into fighting and bloodshed. After a particularly noisy night, with a pall of smoke hanging over the city, the sound of firing across the dividing 'Green Line' and gangs of youths roaming the streets looking for more trouble, I called on Tony at breakfast time to see how he was faring.

He was seated alone at one end of a magnificently polished table. A plate of eggs and bacon was before him, he was sipping a cup of coffee, and propped against the marmalade jar was a week-old copy of *The Times*. If any marauding Cypriot had shown his face, I suspect that one cool glance over the top of *The Times* would have sent him speedily on his way. As it was, in the midst of all the shooting and the shouting in that trouble-torn city, I was able to share the most civilised breakfast in Cyprus. Ealing Studios could not have done it better.

'... the most civilised breakfast in Cyprus.'

10 'Do Tell Us About Your Most Embarrassing Moment'

It is the request that nearly always comes at the end of a talk, and nearly always it catches me unprepared. I can often only rescue myself by confessing that my most embarrassing moment has just arrived, since I cannot recall any other. But of course there have been many – live broadcasting is fraught with them. I set down some of them now, not only because it is a properly chastening experience to be reminded of these disasters, but because I should in future be able to remember one when I am asked that question again.

There are many moments during the hurly-burly of live interviews when one slips up over a name or a title. Sir John Biggs-Davison, for instance, was introduced as 'Mr' for some time after he was knighted; he was as tolerant about that as he was about being called Biggs-Davidson, a constant pitfall for the unwary presenter. Lady Fiennes, wife of the intrepid Sir Ranulph, was regularly referred to as Lady Virginia until somebody explained the correct mode of address for the wife of a baronet, as opposed to the daughter of a peer. And on one dreadful morning I completely forgot the name of Laurie Macmillan, the newsreader who was sitting opposite me, and having got as far as 'Here is our review of the papers read by ...' I had to search desperately through the scripts to find out who she was.

My most disastrous slip-up over a name involved Baroness Phillips, who came in after the death of Lady Isobel Barnett to talk about the sad events which had led up to it. Needless to say, it was a sombre and very serious interview. At the end of it I said simply, 'Thank you, Lady Barnett.' By the time I realised the ghastly mistake, the next interview was being introduced. I had to wait an agonising three minutes before I could apologise, and by then the phones were already buzzing.

Great embarrassments can occur when an outside line breaks down in the middle of an interview or even at the start of one. The more distinguished the interviewee, the more embarrassing the breakdown can be. There are few things more disconcerting than to read a long introduction, address the first penetrating question, then just get a deathly silence in response.

Sometimes it is because the person cannot hear anything at the other end, and he is quite likely to shout unexpectedly, 'Is anybody there?' or 'When are we going to do this interview?' He gets more and more frustrated as he thinks he has been left deserted and forgotten, while the whole nation listens to his exasperated cries. Sometimes it is the other way round; he can hear us but we cannot hear him. In such cases we may well have given up and be moving on to the next item while, unknown to us, the poor chap is talking away enthusiastically into thin air.

Either way, feathers can be ruffled and tempers frayed. In one such mishap, for instance, the line went down during an interview with a well-known trade union leader. When we eventually made contact again, I tentatively enquired if he could hear me. 'Of course I can hear you,' he snapped. Then the line went down again. It took a long time to convince him we had not done it on purpose.

'He gets more and more frustrated as he thinks he has been left deserted and forgotten ...'

This sort of thing naturally delights the listener, however embarrassing it may be to us; it is always fun to see other people slipping on banana skins, real or metaphorical. Sometimes we have to laugh ourselves. There was one memorable exchange during the 1980 general election when I was talking to a Parliamentary colleague, John Sargeant, in the radio car. Suddenly it all went quiet. 'Have I lost you?' I enquired. 'Not at all,' said John, ever so slightly huffily. 'I just stopped so you could ask me another question.'

It all proves that it is live and really happening. If you cheat and pretend that something is live when it is actually recorded, then you deserve all the embarrassment you get if things go wrong. Happily the 'Today' team always plays fair, but there was a time when our colleagues from the sports department sometimes addressed a question to an apparently live contributor, then played a pre-recorded answer. We always looked forward to the day when the tape was played at double speed and they had to explain why some sturdy football manager or cricket captain was suddenly speaking in a high falsetto. Fortunately for them, the studio managers on the tape machines never let them down.

On one occasion I was unlucky myself, though the embarrassment was suffered not by me but by my wife, Pat. I was sent on an assignment to Ethiopia, and during some preliminary research we discovered that one of the ancient savage customs of the country was for a victorious chief to remove vital parts of his defeated enemy's anatomy and wear them as ornaments. I assured Pat that this practice must have long since ceased. It so happened, however, that the first tape I sent back from Ethiopia was accidently played at double speed. My voice rose two octaves – and Pat nearly died!

❖ ❖ ❖

There are some mornings when an entire programme can become a monumental embarrassment. One stumbles over the headlines and gets a fit of coughing during the weather forecást. The live interviews tail off into incoherence or go on far too long, the cues which looked so crisp and witty when they were written at six in the morning sound limp and fatuous when they are eventually read, and the off-the-cuff jokes should have been kept well out of sight up the sleeve.

Even the motoring flashes can prove treacherous. I recall a lorry loaded with *jam* turned over on a *slip* road. We had no end of a jolly time with that one, you may be sure, until someone eventually phoned to tell us the driver was dead.

The worst morning in recent memory combined several such horrors with a few unexpected extras thrown in. It was a morning where we actually had something quite funny to say to fill thirty seconds, and never got a chance to say it because 'Thought for the Day' over-ran. Interviewees failed to materialise at the right time, so for twenty minutes it was an all-Timpson programme, with Brian mooching about in the corridor waiting for someone to talk to, then for the next twenty it was all-Redhead, while I mooched about waiting for mine. Eventually, to avoid it becoming too lop-sided, we were forced to swop cues.

This is a process which any presenter detests. With a straightforward, factual cue into an ordinary news story there is no great problem; one cannot incorporate much of one's personal talents into a line like 'Now more about the economic Summit'. The difficulties arise over the lighter items, where we may well have laboured mightily to produce an apt metaphor, a telling turn of phrase, even a gentle ho-ho. To part with such gems and hear them mangled by one's bewildered colleague, who has not had a chance to grasp their full subtlety, is like a racehorse trainer seeing his star mount being ridden by Cyril Smith.

Thus if we are reporting a drop in bingo attendances and we are poised to say 'Eyes up for an empty house', or if we are introducing a flea map of the British Isles and we want to suggest it would be useful to itch-hikers, it can be very frustrating to be denied the opportunity and to have our brainchildren adopted by someone else. We are therefore inclined to cling to this kind of cue with a terrible tenacity. There are times, though, when a swop cannot be avoided.

It happened on this particular morning. I had written a cue about a deer cull in the New Forest. Casting about in the early hours for something different to say about culling, it occurred to me that, instead of shooting the deer, in this technological age we might develop some sort of techniculler. It was only a throwaway line which might have evoked a gentle response at the odd breakfast table. The fates decreed, however, that Brian had to read it instead. I resigned myself to its loss.

It was not to be. Brian, knowing how I had laboured over this puny pun, decided to give it the full treatment. He read part of the cue, which explained how half the deer population of the New Forest was about to be slaughtered, then announced, quite devastatingly, 'This is where John wants to tell a joke!'

Nothing had been further from my mind. To toss in the techni-culler line as an aside was one thing; to have it proclaimed as my personal reaction to the killing off of defenceless animals was quite another. Had I been more unscrupulous I would merely have said I had no idea what he was talking about, and left him to get out of that. As it was, I blurted out this now quite appalling jest in all its hideous offensiveness. Animal-lovers throughout the country reached for their pens and their telephones. Had they seen my blushes, perhaps they would have shown me the compassion I apparently so lacked myself.

❖ ❖ ❖

That morning of embarrassment did not end there. The classic disaster was yet to come.

It had been planned that for a little light relief at the end of the programme I should interview a distinguished French couturier who happened to be passing through London. By

91

'Today' standards on a dull day, that was reason enough for talking to him – because he was there. But by all accounts he was quite a remarkable character. As well as his dress designing, he ran expensive flower shops, he was into exclusive furniture, natty neckties and exotic perfumes, and he owned the most lavish restaurant in Paris. He now intended to open a similar luxury establishment for the high-class gourmet in that unlikeliest of centres for decadent millionaires, Peking. Such a bizarre project seemed well worth a chat. Certainly his English public relations lady made it all sound great. Nobody had actually talked to the couturier himself.

A couple of minutes before the interview I popped out to meet him. 'Good morning,' I said. 'Good morning,' he replied. Those were the last words I recognised for some time.

It was not that he could not speak English – he spoke a great deal of it, at some considerable speed. I am sure that in more reasonable circumstances it would also have been comprehensible. But he had had a late night at an office party, he had not yet had breakfast, the surroundings were obviously strange, the time very limited. As far as I could see at that stage, 'Good morning' was about as far as the interview was going to get.

I did my best. I extended the introduction to include every facet of his varied career, on the principle that the more I said, the less would have to be said by him. I asked very long questions, which I hoped would require only very short replies. I attempted instant translations, a sort of radio with sub-titles, when those replies came. And to be fair, his English improved remarkably once the adrenalin got going, and I gather he came over as the very charming French gentleman one might expect. But the memory will long remain of those heart-sinking moments after that initial 'Good morning', at the end of that thoroughly ghastly programme. Early retirement never looked more attractive.

❖ ❖ ❖

'... the more I said, the less would have to be said by him.'

Some of the greatest embarrassments can be caused by my fellow journalists, in the write-ups they have given 'Today' from time to time. In the main they can be embarrassingly flattering, and nobody in his senses complains about that. One gets used to ignoring the occasional misquotation, the exaggeration, the incorrect fact or figure, for has one not been guilty of many such errors oneself? And any publicity is good publicity, they say, so long as they spell the name right.

Alas, some of them cannot even do that. The problem was understandable in the days of the distinctively named Jack de Manio, who turned up in all sorts of guises from Demarnio to Di Mannio. One might have thought that Timpson would offer less scope for the imagination, but not so. The central 'p' can be amazingly elusive, but admittedly no great harm is done. The real hazards arise when Timpson becomes Simpson. Numerous luncheon club chairpersons have fallen into this trap, and since the member selected to propose the vote of thanks can be the one person in the room who has never heard of 'Today', let alone Timpson, the error is often perpetuated. Again no great damage is done, except perhaps to the ego, and if I am feeling particularly sour I can always counter the introductory remark, 'I am afraid I have never listened to "Today"' with the observation 'I am afraid I have never bought Mr X's sausages' or whatever.

Much greater havoc can be caused when this sort of error appears in a newspaper. The *Birmingham Post*, for instance, caused great confusion when it reported that John Timpson was to present a current affairs programme called 'Assignment' on BBC1 every Sunday night. As I had only recently returned from 'Tonight' and was just getting rehabilitated on Radio 4, this was a singularly embarrassing announcement. It was also embarrassing for John Simpson, my television colleague, who may well have thought that here was another case where the person who has lost the job is always the last to know.

The record for this kind of inaccuracy must be held by a

lady on the *Glasgow Herald*. BBC Scotland had just started its own breakfast programme soon after Robert Robinson had left us, and acrimonious correspondence broke out in the Scottish Press. The *Herald* columnist then produced this gem: 'Addicts of "Today" who look back with nostalgia to the days of Robert Robinson will be disappointed to know that even if the programme was brought back, Robinson would be absent. He left two or three months ago and his place has been taken by Jim Pimpson.' I could not resist assuring the writer that, while anyone with a name like Jim Pimpson would always be welcome on 'Today', if she actually meant me then any 'addict' could tell her I had been presenting the programme long before Bob even joined it.

By far the greatest embarrassment my Press colleagues have caused me started with a phone call from a gossip columnist on one of the national papers. He casually enquired if I was still living with Roz Hanby, the blue-eyed beauty who used to appear in all those British Airways commercials, saying she would take great care of us. It was the sort of question which made 'Have you stopped beating your wife?' comparatively straightforward.

The fellow seemed quite positive about this entirely non-existent liaison and was obviously unconvinced by my increasingly hysterical assurances that I had been happily married for thirty years and had no plans not to remain so. Nor indeed had I ever even met the lovely Ms Hanby. Finally I assured him that the slightest suggestion in print of some romantic attachment between us would bring down a hail of writs upon his wretched head.

I knew that such a threat has little impact on these chaps, and indeed may merely egg them on, so the next twenty-four hours, waiting for his paper to appear, were the worst I have spent for many a year. Once something like that has been published, no amount of denials or legal actions can

quite undo the damage. While it was vaguely compli-
mentary to be associated with such an obviously desirable
young woman, the repercussions were too appalling to
contemplate.

Happily the story never appeared. Instead, several
months later, another paper revealed that Ms Hanby's
romance was with a totally different BBC man whose name
vaguely resembled mine. It led to this comment in *Girl
About Town* magazine: 'This revelation must come as a
great relief to the ever-professional John Timson (sic) who
presents Radio 4's "Today". For about a year ago, certain
elements of the less reputable parts of Fleet Street were
pursuing poor Timson (still sic), announcing that he was
having an affair with the delightful Roz. "Are you sure
you've got the right man?" asked the unhappy Timson (sic
again – at least he was consistent). The newshounds
reckoned that the blameless Timson (ah well) was just
covering up. Now they know.'

The final sequel took place a year after that, when I
actually met Roz Hanby in the 'Today' studio. She was
leaving British Airways to go into television, and came in to
talk about it. The poor girl was as embarrassed as I was, and
somewhat apologetic that I had got involved. She turned
out to be just as delightful as she looked in the commercials,
and we got along famously. Now, no doubt, that gossip
columnist will be on the telephone again.

❖   ❖   ❖

The ultimate embarrassment, I know, will come when this
book appears. I shall be reminded of all the incidents and
people and correspondence I should have included but
forgot, and no doubt reproached for some of those I did
remember and should have forgotten.

We once discussed on 'Today' a *British Medical Journal*
suggestion that people should write their own obituaries,
and I was asked what I would like in mine. To the critics I can
only quote it again here: AT LEAST HE CAME OUT ON TIME.